Off We Go!

BOOK ONE

KENNETH ANDERSON

Illustrated by Madeleine Robinson

HULTON EDUCATIONAL PUBLICATIONS

ISBN 0 7175 0303 8

First published 1964 *by Hulton Educational Publications Ltd., Raans Road, Amersham, Bucks.*
Reprinted 1968
Reprinted 1971
Revised edition 1973
Reprinted 1973
Reprinted 1975
Reprinted 1976
Text set in 14 *pt. Times New Roman, printed by photolithography, and bound in*
Great Britain at The Pitman Press, Bath

CONTENTS

1 LETTERS OF THE ALPHABET

Here are the **capital** letters:

A   B   C   D   E   F   G   H   I

J   K   L   M   N   O   P   Q   R

S   T   U   V   W   X   Y   Z

Here are the **small** letters, but they are in the wrong order:

g   n   p   a   i   m   b   w   c

t   d   j   y   q   h   o   r   z

e   l   s   f   v   u   x   k

Write the **capital** and **small** letters together like this:

A a,   B b,   C c, . . .

[7]

Here are pictures of twenty-six things:

Here are their names:

patch, whip, apple, owl, umbrella, jar, cat, tub, Xmas tree, queen, fan, milk, kite, robin, gun, egg, lamp, dog, ink, hat, zebra, bat, yacht, net, vase, snake.

Write these names in the **same** order as the pictures.

Do it like this:

1. apple.   2. bat.   3. . . .

2 ANIMALS AND BIRDS

Read this little poem:

The cow gives us milk,
And sometimes meat.
The sheep gives us wool,
And mutton to eat.
The pig gives us bacon,
When he's grown fat.
The hen gives us eggs—
How I love her for that!

Now finish these sentences. All the words you **need** are in the poem:

1. We drink ——.
2. The meat of the sheep is called ——?
3. The —— lays eggs for us.
4. Bacon comes from the ——.
5. Some of our clothes are made from ——.
6. The cow gives us milk and ——.

Here are the names of some **animals** and **birds**:

cat   turkey   sheep   duck   goat   dog
gander   bull   goose   cock   hen   cow

Arrange them in two lists like this:

animals	birds
cat	turkey
sheep	. . .
. . .	

3 SENTENCES

Every sentence begins with a capital letter, like this:

We looked at the television.

These sentences are wrong:

1. the cat chased a bird.
2. all dogs like bones.
3. the moon shone brightly.
4. we have jelly for tea.
5. the light has gone out.
6. there is a rainbow in the sky.
7. the cowboy was shot.
8. we took our radio with us.

Now write the sentences with a **capital letter** at the beginning.

Do it like this:

1. The cat chased a bird.

This is a full stop **.**   This is a question mark **?**

Look at these sentences:

> Harry was late for school.
> Is Mummy home yet?

The first one **tells** you something.   It ends with a **full stop.**

The second one **asks a question.**   It ends with a **question mark.**

Write these sentences out.   Put a full stop or a question mark at the end of each one:

1. How much are those sweets
2. The dog lost his ball
3. Can you come to tea
4. When does the party begin
5. It is raining hard
6. The fire has gone out
7. Do you feel cold
8. We are going home soon
9. The car hit a tree
10. Are the apples ripe

Do it like this:

1. How much are those sweets?
2. The dog lost his ball.

[11]

4 VOWELS

(A) B C D (E) F G H (I)

J K L M N (O) P Q R

S T (U) V W X Y Z

The five letters ringed round are called **vowels.**

All the other letters are called **consonants.**

Write out the full alphabet in capital letters. Draw a **ring** round each vowel and a **line** under each consonant.

Begin like this:

(A) B C D

Look at these words:

spot	stamp	slave	scrub	read	stick
spoil	green	spend	grin	soot	round

Put the words in two lists like this:

one vowel	two vowels
spot	slave
stamp	read

[12]

5 a AND an

Look at these pictures:

    a ball   **an** elephant   **an** orange   **a** house

We say **a** ball and **a** house. **A** comes before words which begin with **consonants**.

We say **an** elephant and **an** orange. **An** comes before words which begin with vowels.

a) Write out these words, and put **a** or **an** in front of each:

bat	fan	egg	ant	cup
girl	uncle	table	Eskimo	owl
pipe	inkwell	towel	aunt	ship
elbow	flower	overcoat	pram	organ

b) Now write out this passage, and put either **a** or **an** into each of the spaces:

  , I saw —— squirrel scamper up —— oak tree. He sat on —— branch and started nibbling at —— piece of bark,

[13]

which he held between his paws. Suddenly —— owl which was resting close to the trunk let out —— angry screech. With —— great leap and —— whisk of his tail, the squirrel took to the air. In —— moment he was clinging to the madly swinging twig of —— ash tree which grew close by.

6 ANIMAL FRIENDS

On the opposite page is a picture of a dog holding a bottle of milk in his mouth. He is feeding a fawn, which is a baby deer. Very many people keep dogs as pets, but some dogs have to work. You all know how farmers and policemen have dogs to help them. Many blind people have dogs which lead them safely across busy roads, and help them to get to and from work.

Now think very hard and try to remember some of the other clever things you have heard about dogs doing. Then write **six** sentences of your own about **dogs.**

[15]

7 TELLING A STORY

Each set of pictures below tells a story. The sentences tell you what happened in words, but they are in the **wrong order**. In each case write the sentences in the **same order** as the **pictures**:

1.

She had her breakfast.
Then she went to school.
Susan got up.

2.

A policeman held up the traffic.
The children crossed the road.
Some children waited at the kerb.

[16]

Now write **three** sentences of your own, describing how you:

1. Get ready to go out in the rain.
2. Get changed for a P.E. lesson.
3. Get dressed for a party.
4. Get ready for bed.

8 MORE SENTENCES

Every sentence must **make sense.**

This is a sentence:

> John and Mary went to the park.

This **is not** a sentence:

> Joan and Pat like.

Now look at these:

1. Peter lost sixpence.
2. Mary likes cats.
3. Harry has cut his.
4. My new book is about.
5. The girl wore a blue.
6. The space-man went into orbit.
7. The party was on Dick's.
8. Playtime was over.
9. The roses had a beautiful.
10. Harry fell through the ice.

[17]

Which five are **sentences**?   Write them out.

Which five are **not** sentences?   Add a word from this list to each, and write them out so that they **are** sentences:

birthday   scent   knee   dress   cowboys

In the little story which follows, the capital letters and full stops have been left out.   Read it carefully, then write it out **correctly,** putting in the capital letters and full stops.   There are **five** sentences:

One night the sound of the wind woke me up it was howling round the chimneys the window panes were rattling I could hear the trees being tossed about in the garden a rattle and a crash told me that a slate had come off the roof.

Now write down a passage of **five** sentences describing a windy day.

9 MORE ABOUT VOWELS

a   e   i   o   u

Put the right vowel in each of the spaces:

1. The c—t caught a mouse.
2. Baby sleeps in a c—t.
3. Mother l—t me play in the garden.
4. Tom c—t his finger.
5. Father l—t the bonfire.
6. Please l—ck the door.
7. Jack has a p—ck of cards.
8. The cat l—cks her paw.
9. The robin tried to p—ck the sparrow.
10. I had the good l—ck to win a prize.

Each word in this list has **one** vowel:

pin	pan	bat	sung	sang
suck	bit	lot	bell	met
fell	fold	sun	bun	set
sing	song	sick	sock	mat
rat	milk	went	pat	but

Now put the words into five lists by looking at the vowel in each one.

Do it like this:

a	e	i	o	u
pan	set	pin	lot	bun

[19]

10 NAMES WHICH BEGIN WITH CAPITAL LETTERS

Copy these words:

John Smith   Sheila Brown   Robert Banks   Paul Jones
London   Brighton   Bristol   Liverpool   Kent
Devon   Lancaster   Sussex   Yarmouth   Yorkshire

All these words begin with **capital letters** because they are the names of **people** or **places.**

Now write these words:

town	boy	girl	street	mountain
mother	father	river	country	child
teacher	garden	man	woman	pencil

These words begin with **small** letters because they are **not** names which belong to only **one** person or place.

1. Now put these words into two lists, showing whether they begin with **capital** letters or **small** letters:

flower	England	carpet	Hastings	John
brush	Richard	Sally	France	radio
cousin	aunt	Dickens	Essex	wall
Scotland	Henry	leaf	cupboard	uncle

Write the list of words which begin with capital letters on the **left** of your page, and the list of words which begin with small letters on the **right.**

11 [ch] AND [sh]

Write out these sentences, putting **ch** or **sh** in the spaces:

1. Tom likes fi.. and ..ips.
2. Please ..ow me a bir.. tree.
3. The ..air had a ru.. seat.
4. Most of the toys in the ..op cost too mu...
5. I do wi.. I was ri...
6. The driver had to wa.. the coa...
7. Everyone began to ..eer as the ..ip sailed.
8. ..op up the meat and put it in the di...
9. We found some ..ells on the bea...
10. It is quite ..illy in the ..ed.

Now do the same with this passage:

I lifted the lat.. and went into the ..ed. I swit..ed on the light and went to the tool ..elf. Taking down a ..arp ..isel, I put it in an old ..oe box, and took it in to my father. He then ..owed me how to ..ip out the groove, and told me how he once had to have his finger stit..ed up through being careless.

Have you ever hurt yourself through being careless or doing something you had been told not to? If so, write about it. If you cannot remember anything happening to you, make up a little story.

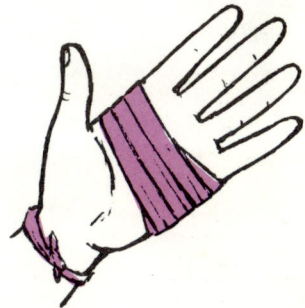

[22]

12 ON THE FARM

The picture opposite shows a village. You can see the church and some of the houses, but the most important thing is the large farm in the centre. Built onto the farmhouse are barns for storing hay and other animal foods. There are sheds where the farmer keeps his machines. Also there is a cow-shed where the cows live in the winter, and go twice a day to be milked. No doubt hens, ducks and geese live in the two farm-yards you can see. In the larger one is a dutch barn where more hay is stored. The round tower near the front is a silo, where chopped-up hay is kept for winter. The three square towers to the left of the farm are oast houses, where the farmer dries his hops. He sells them for beer-making. Hops grow on strings tied to tall poles. Can you see the poles? There are many other things to see, although the cattle and sheep are out in the fields which you cannot see in the picture.

Think of all the jobs the farmer, his wife and his men have to do. Suppose you went to spend a holiday on this farm. What sort of things would you like to do? How could you help? What is it like in the village? Think carefully, then write **eight** sentences about "A Farm Holiday".

13 HOMES OF ANIMALS

The dog's in his basket,
The bird's in her nest,
And Jack's in his stable,
The place he likes best.
The cows are locked up
In their warm, dry shed,
And I am tucked down
In my own little bed.

Now write the answers to these questions about the poem. Each answer should be a complete sentence:

1. Where is the dog?
2. Who is in the nest?
3. What kind of animal is Jack?
4. Where are the cows?
5. Where am I?

Now make up a poem of your own about animals and the countryside. Here are some words which might help you:

rabbit	sheep	fox	hive	sparrow	
owl	bees	hen	hutch	sty	fold
pig	mouse	hoot	hole	coop	feather

14 CHRISTIAN NAMES AND SURNAMES

John Parks   **Joan** Parks

These children are twins.   Their Christian names are in **bold type,** their surname in ordinary type.   Here are some of their friends:

William Jones   Peter Hunt   Jean Wilson
Christine Robins   Paul Mills   Susan Smith
Keith Andrews   Mary Spencer

Now arrange their names in three lists like this:

Girls' Christian Names	Boys' Christian Names	Surnames
Jean	William	Jones

Here are the names of two families:

Mr. Edward Heath   Mr. Stephen Hill
Mrs. Brenda Heath   Mrs. Sheila Hill
Pauline Heath   Robert Hill
Frederick Heath   Valerie Hill
Jean Heath   Brian Hill

Now finish these sentences:

[25]

1. Mr. Heath's Christian name is ——.
2. Mrs. Hill's Christian name is ——.
3. Pauline's surname is ——.
4. Valerie's surname is ——.
5. The Christian name of Jean's brother is ——.

Now write out the full Christian names and surname of all the people in your family, and then write about **six** sentences about them. Do not forget yourself.

You may start like this:

There are —— people in my family including my father and mother. ————

15 ee AND ea

seed	beef	sheet	street	speed
seat	beat	stream	clean	cheat

Learn how to spell these words.

Now write out these sentences, putting in the missing letters:

1. Sally fell into the str..m.
2. Fred b..t Colin at chess.
3. Jet planes fly at high sp..d.
4. Father bought some grass s..d.
5. The sh..t was blown off the line.
6. Kate's hands were always cl..n.
7. The str..t was flooded after the storm.

[26]

8. Jean called Pam a ch..t.
9. Mother bought a joint of b..f.
10. I had a front s..t on the bus.

Now write out this passage putting either **ee** or **ea** into each of the spaces:

I was playing on the b —— ch when I heard a scr —— m. A little boy had fallen into d —— p water. His mother, who had been f —— ding her baby, pulled him out. She saw something gl —— ming on the sand under the water. It was a brooch with a gr —— n stone shaped like a b —— tle in it. She thought it was only a ch —— p one, but she took it to the police station. Nobody s —— med to have lost it, so after thr —— months she was told she could k —— p it.

Now write a story of your own, of not less than **six** sentences, called "Found on the Seashore".

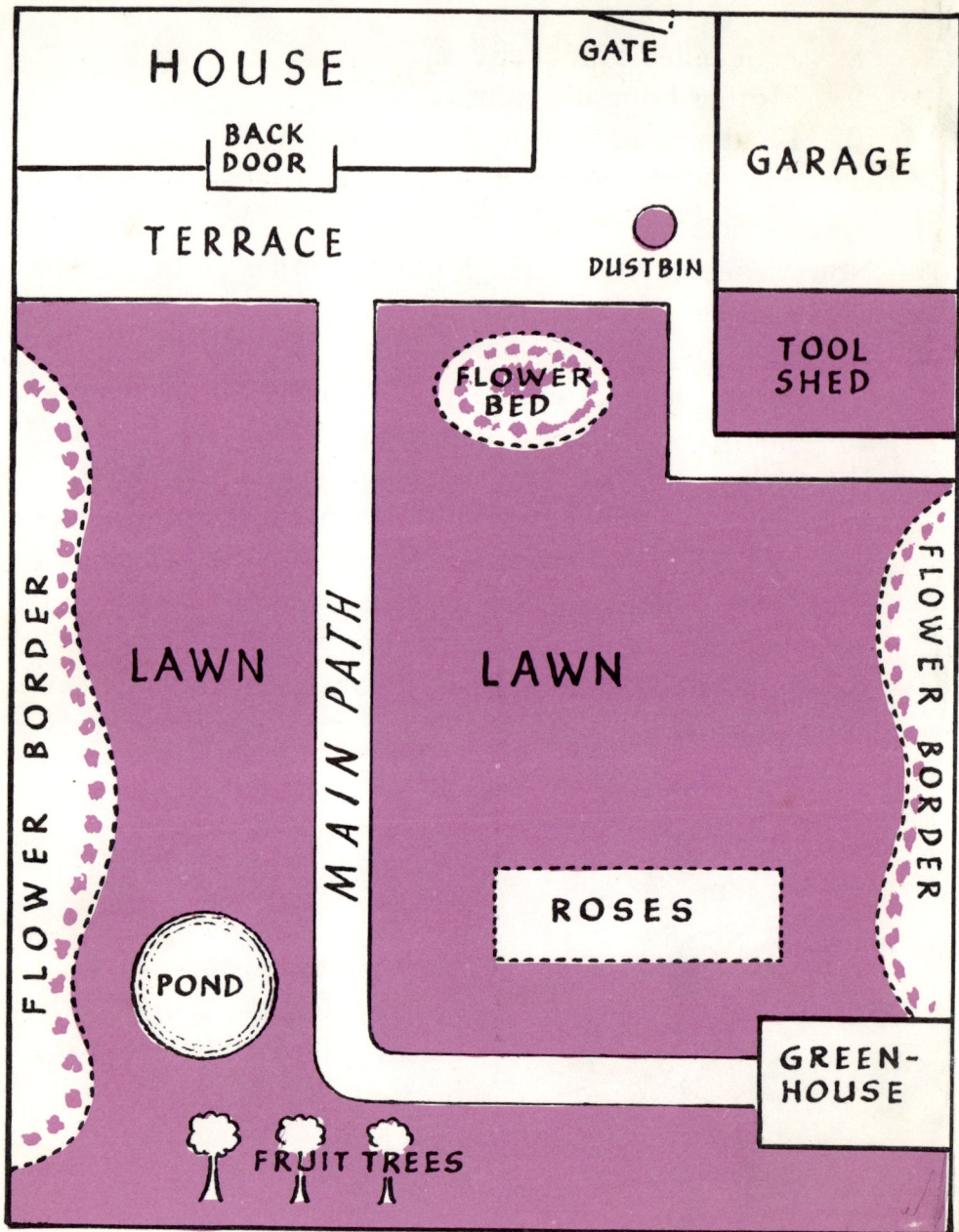

HOUSE

BACK
DOOR

GATE

GARAGE

TERRACE

DUSTBIN

TOOL
SHED

FLOWER
BED

LAWN

MAIN PATH

LAWN

FLOWER BORDER

FLOWER BORDER

ROSES

POND

GREEN-
HOUSE

FRUIT TREES

[28]

16 A GARDEN

On the opposite page you can see the plan of a garden. Look at it carefully, then write out these sentences, choosing the correct word from the bracket in each case:

1. The main path leads to the (toolshed greenhouse).
2. The rose bed is (square oblong) in shape.
3. The flower bed is (oval round) in shape.
4. There is a flower border on (one each) side of the garden.
5. The flower borders have (straight curved) edges.
6. The fruit trees are at the (side bottom) of the garden.
7. The pond is (circular oval) in shape.
8. The lawn is covered with (flowers grass).
9. The tool shed is (beside behind) the garage.
10. Looking from the house down the garden, the dustbin is on the (left right).

Now think about your own garden, or the garden of somebody you know, and write about it. Think of the games you could play, or how you could help to keep it tidy. Also mention some of the flowers you could plant in the beds and borders.

[29]

17 b AND d

Look at these words:

bath   bell   daddy   brick   drip   boat
donkey brim   drum   bottle   doll   desk

Now put them in two lists like this:

b	d
bath	daddy

Do the same with these words, but change the capital letters to **small** letters:

DRINK   DROP   BEAM   DART   BIKE
BIRD   DEN   DREAM BELT   BANGLE
            BUMP   DATE

Do it like this:

b	d
beam	drink

Now write out these sentences, changing the **capital** letters in the words in bold type to **small** letters:

1. A **BABOON** is a **WILD** animal.
2. A **DEAD BIRD** was lying in the **DITCH**.
3. The **DONKEY** was eating **DANDELION** plants in the **PADDOCK**.
4. Put the **DEAD** flowers in the **RUBBISH BIN**.
5. Put the soap flakes in the **DISH**, and we can **BLOW BUBBLES**.

[30]

18 WORDS WHICH RHYME

cat	day	walk	cart	date	fight
mat	play	talk	dart	late	light

Words which have endings which sound the same are said to **rhyme**.

Arrange these words into **pairs** which **rhyme**:

book	sweep	near	corn	nail	spout
weed	tall	boat	bay	shout	long
cook	tail	song	horn	dear	down
coat	town	peep	feed	hay	fall

Do it like this:

book — cook   sweep — peep

Each of the words below will rhyme with one of the words printed in bold type in the passage which follows. Put it into the right space:

skirt   dark   wall   fair   back

Tom wore a white **shirt** and Joan wore a blue ——. Her **hair** was long and ——, and streamed in the wind as they played. But soon their **ball** went over the garden ——. **Mrs. Black** threw it ——, but then they decided to go to the **park** before it got ——.

[31]

Now write **six** sentences describing what they did in the park.

19 there AND their

My house is over **there**.
There was once a king who had three sons.
The boys put on **their** caps.

These sentences show you how to use **there** and **their**.

Remember that **their** is always followed by the **name** of something.

Now put either **their** or **there** into the spaces in these sentences:

1. Our school is over ——.
2. —— was a fly in the spider's web.
3. They waved to —— teacher.
4. The children lost —— way.
5. —— was one child missing.
6. It was cold, but —— was no wind.
7. Do they all know —— tables?
8. The birds are sitting on —— eggs.
9. Tom went to the fair and saw Harry ——.
10. Once upon a time —— was a wicked witch.

[32]

Now do the same with this passage:

If —— mother will let them, Betty and John are going to have some of —— friends to tea next Sunday. —— will be a cake for Betty's birthday, and of course —— will be jelly and ice-cream as well. If —— friends get —— early enough, they can watch Television for a while before having —— tea.

20 PUNCTUATION

You have learned that all sentences begin with a **capital letter** and end with a **full stop** or **question mark.** Also that names of **people** and **places** begin with a capital letter.

Now write out the sentences below as they should be. This is called **punctuation.** There is **one** thing to put right in each sentence:

1. the man is selling plants.
2. The baker left two loaves
3. May I go into the garden
4. I saw peter in the park.
5. I am going to have tea with mary.
6. the clock has just struck ten.
7. Were you late for school this morning
8. did you read that book I lent you?
9. Most boys like playing football
10. I am going swimming with sheila.

Begin like this:

1. The man is selling plants.

[33]

Now write this passage out correctly as **five** sentences:

I always enjoy a visit to our local street market there are dozens of stalls there most of them sell fruit or vegetables others sell plants or flowers the most interesting ones sell toys, games and colourful balloons.

Look at the picture of a street market above. Suppose you visited a strange street market like this with your parents, and became lost. Describe what happened to you in at least **six** sentences.

[34]

21 MORE THAN ONE

One tree   One bird   One train
Two trees   **Three** birds   **Ten** trains

s on the end of a word means **more than one.**

Look at these pictures:

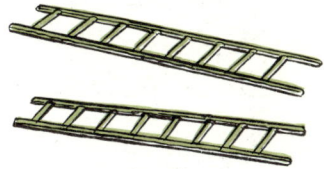

Complete each of the sentences below by choosing a word from this list:

house   pipe   ladders   flower   pipes   wheels
houses   ladder   wheel   bird   flowers   birds

1. There are five ——.
2. There are three ——.
3. There are two ——.
4. There are four ——.
5. There are six ——.
6. There are seven ——.

[35]

one church	one fox	one glass	one wish
two churches	**six** foxes	**four** glasses	**three** wishes

When a word ends in **ch, x, s,** or **sh,** we put **es** on the end to show there is **more than one.**

Change the words in bold type in this passage to show that there is **more than one:**

Harry has been to three football **match** in the last month. He loves above all to see George Best making his **dash** down the wing, spraying **pass** to his team-mates all over the field, and making perfect **cross** from the corner flag to his inside forwards. At home he has four **box** of football match programmes that he has collected.

Harry collected football programmes. Write **six** sentences about any collections that you have made.

[36]

22 ur AND ir

burn	turn	churn	hurt	curl
girl	bird	shirt	skirt	circus

Learn how to spell these words.

Now write out these sentences, putting in the missing letters:

1. The blue-tit is a pretty b..d.
2. The farmer knocked over a ch..n of milk.
3. T..n right at the cross-roads.
4. Damp wood will not b..n.
5. Do you like Jean's new sk..t?
6. May we go to the c..cus?
7. Jack tore his new white sh..t.
8. Nobody was h..t in the crash.
9. The g..l jumped for joy.
10. The baby had a big c..l over his forehead.

Now do the same with this passage:

Jane was a lucky g — l. For her b — thday she had a red sk — t, a leather p — se, and a n — se's uniform. She was also going to be taken to the c — cus. But that afternoon, she was passing the ch — ch, when she tripped and h — t her ankle. Mother put a f — m bandage on it,

[37]

and she was able to walk all right. That evening she set off for the Big Top almost b — sting with excitement.

Suppose that you were Jane. Write an account of some of the things you saw at the circus.

23 WHAT AM I?

Look at these four sentences:

> I am a very wise bird.
> My eyes are large and round.
> After dark I catch many rats and mice.
> I am an —— .

The word missing from the last sentence is **owl**. So the last sentence should be: I am an owl.

Write out these groups of sentences putting in the missing word in each case:

1. I am a friendly little bird.
   My picture is often on Christmas cards.
   You know me by my red breast.
   I am a —— .

2.   I have soft, warm fur.
     When it gets dark, I go out hunting.
     Mice are afraid of my sharp claws, and so are birds.
     I am a —— .

Now write groups of **four** sentences, like those above, about:

(a) A lamb   (b) A fox   (c) A dog
(d) A mouse   (e) A budgerigar

24 NUMBERS

Here are the numbers 1—12, with their names:

1	2	3	4	5	6
one	**two**	**three**	**four**	**five**	**six**

7	8	9	10	11	12
seven	**eight**	**nine**	**ten**	**eleven**	**twelve**

Now put the missing word in each of these sentences:

1. On each hand we have —— fingers and —— thumb.
2. There are —— days in a week.
3. You get —— eggs when you buy a dozen.
4. The lucky number is —— .
5. There are —— gloves in a pair.
6. The first number with two figures is ——.
7. You have —— toes on each foot.
8. The next even number after four is ——.

[39]

9. —— new half-pence are the same as four new pence.
10. The next two odd numbers after seven are ——
   and —— .

25 VERBS

kick	jump	bark	talk
sleep	think	throw	sing

These are words which tell us what people or things **do.**
They are called **verbs.**

Sometimes verbs have **ing** on the end, like this:

kicking	jumping	barking	talking
sleeping	thinking	throwing	singing

Use these verbs ending in **ing** to write a sentence about
each of these pictures:

Tom

Jane

Rover

Heather

Richard

Paul

Susan

Hilary

Do it like this:

1. Tom is kicking.

Here are some pictures of things which you know well.

gun   spider   bell   duck   ball

sun   fire   boat   chimney   kettle

Here are some more verbs:

smoking	shining	swimming	boiling	sailing
burning	spinning	bouncing	ringing	firing

Now use these verbs to write a sentence about each thing. The verbs are **not** in the same order as the pictures.

[41]

26 |here| AND |hear|

Please come **here.**

Did you **hear** a whisper?

These sentences show you how to use **here** and **hear.**

Remember that you **hear** things with your **ear.**

Now write out these sentences, and choose the right word from the bracket in each.

1. We came (here   hear) to play cricket.
2. Brian did not (here   hear) the bell.
3. I did not (here   hear) what you said.
4. Mary came (here   hear) to borrow a book.
5. (Here   Hear) is the bat I told you about.
6. The boys pretended not to (here   hear) the teacher.
7. No children are allowed in (here   hear).
8. He could not (here   hear) what Jack was saying.
9. Fred looked (here   hear), there and everywhere for his cap.
10. I (here   hear) you were top of the class.

Now write out this short passage, putting either **here** or **hear** into each space:

My father used to come —— during the summer to —— the nightingales singing.   If he got —— before ten o'clock, he might —— two or three of them, but if he arrived —— later, he might not —— any at all.

[42]

27 WHAT ARE THEY DOING?

1. Keith   2. Janet   3. Mr. Jones

1. Keith is playing football.
2. Janet is feeding the ducks.
3. Mr. Jones is reading the newspaper.

These three sentences describe what is happening in the pictures.

Write a sentence like this about each of these pictures:

Paul   Helen   Sam   Kenneth   Mrs. Smith

[43]

| Tom | Rover | Tibbles | Joan | Christine |

Here are some **names** which will help you:

cricket   washing   apple   tree   cat
doll   garden   puzzle   kite   television

Here are some **verbs** which will help you:

watching   doing   playing   hanging   watering
chasing   flying   dressing   climbing   eating

28 WORDS WHICH HAVE tch

Look at these words carefully; then write them out.

Do not forget the **t** in front of the **ch.**

match   catch   latch   witch   hutch   Dutch
stitch   sketch   watch   kitchen scratch   stretch

Now write out these sentences, putting in the missing letters:

1. Susan made a ske... of a Du... house.
2. We love to wa... the rabbits in their hu....

[44]

3. The fairy promised to ca... the wi....
4. The ma...es are in the ki...en.
5. I scra...ed my hand on the la....
6. Do not stre... the sti...es too far.

Now do the same with this passage:

A large clump of weeds hid the dry di ——. In went
Andrew with a thump, straight into a pa —— of nettles.
He came out clu —— ing his knees, which were covered
with stings. Just then the bu —— er came by in his van,
and gave Andrew a lift home. He gave him some butter-
sco —— too, which made him feel much better.

Now write down what you think Andrew told his mother
when she asked what had happened.

29 WRITING SENTENCES IN ORDER

Each set of pictures tells a story. There is a sentence
about each picture. Write the sentences in the **same order**
as the **pictures**:

They go to school together.
Peter leaves his house.
He calls for his friend.

Begin like this: 1.   Peter leaves his house.

She put the mixture in the tin.
Jill mixed up the flour, sugar and butter.
Then she put the tin in the oven.

Then they had a shower and dressed.
They had a good game.
The boys put on their football kit.
After that they sat down to tea.

Now write out three groups of **four** sentences each describing how:

1.   Mary made a cup of tea.
2.   Colin made a sand-castle on the beach.
3.   Susan rescued a young bird which had fallen from its nest.

[46]

30 WORDS INSTEAD OF PICTURES

Here are pictures of twelve things or people, with their names:

taxi   cows   tree   driver   trolley   gate

porter   rack   door   signal-box   train   cases

Write out the story, putting the right **word** instead of each picture:

As the  passed the  we took our

 down from the . When it stopped

we opened the  and called a  He put

our luggage on a  and wheeled it to a

The  took our things, and we set out for the farm.

[47]

As we arrived, the  were coming out of the

 to be milked. Outside the farmhouse was the

tallest  we had ever seen.

Here are some questions about the story:

1. When did we take our cases down?
2. Where were the cases?
3. Who did we call when we opened the door?
4. What did he put the luggage on?
5. Where were we going?
6. How did we get there from the station?
7. Where were the cows going?
8. Why did the tree interest us?

Here are the answers, but in a different order. Write them in the **same order** as the questions:

a. We were going to a farm.
b. The cows were going to be milked.
c. The cases were on the rack.
d. We called a porter.
e. It was the tallest tree we had ever seen.
f. We went to the farm by taxi.
g. When we passed the signal-box.
h. He put our luggage on a trolley.

31 of AND off

A bag **of** sugar please.

Mind how you get **off** the train.

These two sentences show you how to use **of** and **off.**

Now write out these sentences, choosing the right word from the brackets:

1. Have you ever heard (of   off) Mozart?
2. Two bars (of   off) chocolate, please.
3. The boy was let (of   off) with a warning.
4. Nelson is one (of   off) our great heroes.
5. The box fell (of   off) the lorry.
6. He jumped (of   off) the bus before it had stopped.
7. He dived (of   off) the pier.
8. William (of   off) Orange became King William III.
9. The Prince (of   off) Wales will one day be King.
10. The man's hat was blown (of   off) by the gale.

Now write out this short passage, putting either **of** or **off** in each space:

On one —— the wettest days —— the year, Sam fell —— his bicycle when crossing a field. He landed in a puddle —— muddy water near the path. He was not hurt, but it took him a very long time to get the mud —— his clothes.

[49]

32 ALL ABOUT PETS

Jean, Susan and Mary live in the same street. Jean has a dog called Rover, and Susan has a cat whose name is Tinker. Mary, who lives in a flat, has a budgie called Peter. All three girls love their pets, and look after them very well. Jean takes Rover into the park every day, and Susan often plays with Tinker in the garden. Mary is spending a lot of time teaching Peter to talk.

Now fit these words into the sentences which follow:

Mary   Peter   Jean   Tinker   Rover   Susan

1. The owner of the dog is —— .
2. —— is being taught to talk.
3. The cat's name is —— .
4. Tinker belongs to —— .
5. —— is often taken into the park.
6. The girl who lives in a flat is called —— .

Here are some of the **names** of people or things which you can find in the story:

park   Tinker   flat   cat   Mary   budgie
Susan   Rover   pets   dog   garden   Jean

Put them into two lists, one of names beginning with **capital** letters, the other of those beginning with **small** letters.

Begin like this:

Capital letters	Small letters
Tinker	park

In this picture you can see a big beautiful dog called Rex with one of his friends. Write a story, of about **eight** sentences, describing an adventure which Rex and his friends had one summer's day.

Now write **six** sentences about one of your own pets, and make them as interesting as possible. If you do not have a pet of your own, write about the pet you would **like** to have. Do not forget to say how you would look after it and keep it happy.

[51]

33 MAKING SENTENCES

Here are the **names** of ten things:

balloon	windmill	lightning	ice	stars
owl	knife	flowers	spider	fish

Here are ten **verbs**, or **doing words**:

hoots	cuts	bloom	spins	swim
turns	twinkle	flashes	melts	burst

Make short sentences by joining each name with the verb which goes with it best. Write them in the **same order** as the **names.**

Begin like this:

    1. The balloon burst.

Now make each of the sentences you have written into a **longer** sentence by adding to it the most suitable of these endings:

. . . in the sunshine.   . . . with a bang.
. . . in the sea.   . . . in the thunderstorm.
. . . in the garden.   . . . in the woods.
. . . in the sky.   . . . through the butter.
. . . in the wind.   . . . a beautiful web.

Begin like this:

    1. The balloon burst with a bang.

34 b AND d AGAIN

This is a
.lack.oar..

This is a
.ri.ge.

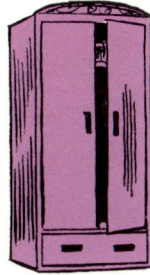

This is a
war.ro.e.

Mary is
.ehin. Tom.

Write out the four sentences above, putting in the missing letters.

Now write out these sentences, choosing the right word from the brackets:

1. The corn is in the (barn   darn).
2. The leaves turn (brown   drown) in autumn.
3. The weather is very (bull   dull).
4. Robin Hood hunted the (beer   deer).
5. The dog was given a (bone   done).
6. The water ran down the (brain   drain).

Now write out these words using **small letters** instead of **capitals**:

CABBAGE	RADISH	CUPBOARD	BIBLE
ABODE	ADDITION	BRAMBLE	DREDGER
DRIBBLE	DRAB	BRIDLE	RIDDLE

35 MORE RHYMING WORDS

wrote	gale	meet	lane	white	calm
goat	tail	wheat	train	night	farm

These pairs of words rhyme, for although their endings are **spelt differently,** they **sound** the **same.**

Arrange these words into pairs which rhyme:

bite	neat	leak	could	tale
bait	rain	vote	fern	gate
sheet	wood	sight	week	stoat
nail	peal	mane	wheel	turn

Do it like this:

bite — sight   neat — sheet

Now complete each of these sentences by choosing from the brackets the word which **rhymes** with the word in bold letters.

1. The driver of the **mail** van looked very (red well pale).
2. The old man (sat stood walked) as long as he **could.**
3. I had a **fright** when I saw the (dark faint white) shape.
4. Nobody would give the **rude** boy any (food water money).
5. The **team** did not (appear seem want) to be ready.
6. Harry's mother wrote a **note** about the lost (cap scarf coat).
7. If we **wait** any longer we shall be (cold late silly).
8. I **beat** Jack in a race down the (street road lane).

[54]

36 WORDS WITH dge

badger	hedge	bridge	dredger	dodge
hedgehog	sledge	judge	ledge	budgie

Write out these sentences, completing the unfinished words:

1. We stood on the b —— watching the d —— at work in the harbour.
2. A b —— r was trying to make the h —— unroll itself.
3. We could see a b —— perched on the window l ——.
4. The s —— hit a stone and crashed into a h ——.
5. The j —— was told that the man had tried to d —— paying his taxes.

Look in your dictionary and find **ten** other words, apart from those above, which have 'dge' in them.

Now write out this passage correctly as **four** sentences:

One winter evening I was watching television my father was out and my mother told me she was going up to the pillar box with a letter I heard the front door close, and a few moments later both light and television went off. I was alone in the darkness.

What happened next? Write **five** sentences about it.

[55]

37 to too two

We are going **to** India by air.
Charles is going **to** work in a factory.

These sentences show you how to use **to**.

It is **too** hot for playing football.
If you go swimming, can I come **too**?

These sentences show you how to use **too**.

There are **two** warships in the bay.

This sentence shows you that **two** is the number.

Now put **to, too,** or **two** in each space in these sentences:
1. If the water is —— hot, put some cold in.
2. We watched —— men playing tennis.
3. Can you come out —— play?
4. —— rockets were fired into space.
5. Is Father coming —— ?
6. May we go —— the football match?
7. I am going —— throw the ball back.
8. —— halves are the same as one whole.
9. The toy boat sank because it was —— heavy.
10. If Tom comes ——, we can have a better game.

38 MATCHING PICTURES AND SENTENCES

These pictures tell the story of a day's outing:

Below is a sentence to describe each picture, but in the **wrong order.**

Write out the sentences in the **same order** as the **pictures:**

a. A real treat followed, because they had an elephant ride.
b. As it was now four o'clock, they went to see the lions fed.
c. Next they went to see the monkeys, which made them laugh.
d. John and Mary waited at the bus-stop with their father.
e. The first animals they saw were the zebras.
f. Then they visited the bears, which were begging for buns.
g. They then had tea at a café before leaving for home.
h. After a long bus ride, they got off at the zoo.

[57]

You have just read about an outing to the Zoo. Now write **eight** sentences of your own, describing an outing which **you** have enjoyed. It can be an outing to a zoo, a large town, a museum, a seaside resort or a famous building. Remember to use capital letters and full stops correctly.

Now write this passage correctly as **five** sentences:

A zoo is a fascinating place that gentle giant the giraffe nibbles at a bunch of leaves nearby vicious tigers roar and snarl as feeding time approaches gusts of laughter show that the chimps are up to their tricks not far away penguins and sea lions gambol in their pool.

39 THE CHILDREN'S ZOO

Look carefully at the picture opposite. It shows animals from a children's zoo being taken for a walk. Now write **eight** interesting sentences about what you can see in the picture.

Here are some words which will help you:

llama	sheep	pony	dog	ladies
path	trees	leaves	fence	wire
walking	bridge	grass	clean	friendly

[58]

[59]

40 ALL ABOUT SCHOOL

A boy was asked some questions about himself. Here are his answers:

1. My name is Peter Smith.
2. I am eight years old.
3. I live at 24, Brent Gardens.
4. I have one brother and two sisters.
5. I go to Burnt Ash Primary School.
6. I am in Class 4.
7. My teacher's name is Miss Kent.
8. I like history best.

Suppose that **you** have been asked the same questions as Peter Smith. Write the answers **you** would give.

A new girl, Amanda Duncan, comes to your school. When she goes home at the end of the day her mother asks her about her new school. Write down in at least **six** sentences what you think Amanda would say.

On the opposite page you can see a photograph taken inside a very modern school which has just been built. It is not divided up into separate classrooms, that is why there is so

much space, and why you can see more than one teacher at work. Can you see why the school is so bright? What are the children doing? Is any of their work on show? Do they have any pets? Can you see any books? Where is the nature table? Find the answers to these questions, and then write **six** sentences about the picture. Then write **four** more saying whether you would like to go to a school like this, and saying why.

[61]

41 WORDS ENDING WITH $\boxed{y}$

One boy	One donkey	One key
Two boys	**Five** donkeys	**Four** keys

These words have a **vowel** in front of the **y**.

When there is **more than one** we put **s** on the end.

One baby	One lady	One lorry
Two babies	**Six** ladies	**Three** lorries

These words have a **consonant** in front of the **y**.

When there is **more than one** we **leave off** the **y** and put **ies.**

Here are some words which usually end in **y** written to show that there is **more than one:**

trays	cities	fairies	pansies	keys
donkeys	countries	storeys	monkeys	babies

Now write out these sentences, changing the words in bold type to show that there is **more than one:**

1. Jill and Diane were dressed as **fairy.**
2. Five **donkey** were giving rides on the sands.
3. Father has lost his bunch of **key.**
4. The **monkey** were impossible to catch.

[62]

5. Most of the **baby** were crying.
6. There are many **pansy** in the garden.
7. England has many great **city.**
8. Most **country** belong to the United Nations.
9. Mother has two silver **tray.**
10. The block of flats had twelve **storey.**

Now turn to your reading book and find ten other **names of things** which end in **y.** Find how to spell them when there is **more than one.** Write out this passage correctly as **four** sentences:

last week we had a holiday from school most of the time we spent playing games in the park we did go out with Mother one day she took us into Mexworthy to buy new blazers.

42 ORDER

These words tell you the **order** of things:

first   second   third   fourth   fifth   sixth
seventh eighth   ninth   tenth   eleventh twelfth

Some children had a maths test.
Over the page you can see the results.

Write a sentence about each child, giving the **order** in which he or she came in the test.

[63]

NAME	MARKS	ORDER
Anne	29	1
Harry	26	2
Susan	25	3
Ellen	21	4
Tom	20	5
Charles	18	6
Dick	16	7
Andrew	15	8
Peter	12	9
Mary	8	10
Joe	7	11
Linda	1	12

Do it like this:

1. Anne was first.
2. Harry was second.

43 w AND wh

who	when	where	why	which
with	went	want	would	were

Here are ten words which you very often need to use. Learn to spell them, and remember that those in the first line begin with **wh**; those in the second line **do not** have an **h.**

Use each of the words to fill a space in these sentences:

1. —— of these two caps is mine?
2. I cycled to the park —— my brother.
3. Three people —— hurt in the accident.
4. Do you —— any more sugar in your tea?
5. —— gave you that stamp?
6. John —— to the dentist's yesterday.
7. —— you help me with these sums, please?
8. Do you know —— the holidays begin?
9. I cannot remember —— I left my raincoat.
10. —— did you hit John like that?

Now make up ten sentences of your own, using each of the words in the **same order** as in the list at the beginning of the exercise.

44 o WHICH SOUNDS LIKE u

The word **come** rhymes with **drum**.
The word **done** rhymes with **sun**.

Here are some more words in which the **o** sounds like a **u**:

some	none	dove	love	above
mother	brother	glove	other	cover

Write out these sentences and put in the missing letters:

1. I l.ve ice-cream, but there was n.ne left in the shop.

[65]

2. My m.ther bought me a pair of gl.ves.
3. My br.ther is one place ab.ve me in class.
4. There is a picture of a d.ve on the c.ver.
5. S.me blue-tits hatched out the .ther day.

Here are twenty words. Arrange them in two lists according to the way in which the **o** is pronounced:

frock	lovely	fodder	dozen	among
governor	modern	hostel	constable	money
body	bolt	front	toddle	recover
cold	long	tongue	polish	problem

Do it like this:

o	u
frock	lovely

45 SENTENCE BUILDING

vase   **flowers**   **garden**

The vase was filled with flowers from the garden.

The group of words in bold type have all been used in the sentence which follows them.

Now use each of these groups in a sentence. You may use them in **any order**:

1. birthday   book   pictures
2. ruler   pen   rubber
3. game   cricket   park

4.	butter	cheese	grocer
5.	cat	bird	bush
6.	shed	tools	father
7.	television	radio	programme
8.	teacher	pencil	knife
9.	book	library	ticket
10.	platform	train	station

Do it like this:

1. On my birthday I was given a book full of nature pictures.

46 SILENT LETTERS

Write out these words:

listen	fasten	write	wrong	wrap	thumb
climb	lamb	know	knot	gnat	gnaw

The letter in bold type is a **silent** letter.

Now write out these sentences, putting in the missing letters:

1. Do you .now how to .rite in code?
2. It is .rong to suck your thum..
3. .rap up the parcel and tie a good .not.
4. We saw the lost lam. clim.ing the hill.
5. Fas.en the window and keep out the .nats.
6. The dog can .naw his bone and lis.en at the same time.

[67]

47 AT HOME

Here are some names of **places** or **things** in your homes

kitchen   hall   bedroom   bathroom   larder

wardrobe   bunker   dining-   garage   shed
                               room

Now use one of these names to finish each of these sentences:

1. We sleep in our —— .
2. We have dinner in the —— .
3. We wash in the —— .
4. Mother cooks in the —— .
5. We hang our hats and coats in the —— .
6. Mother keeps food in the —— .
7. The car is kept in the —— .
8. Our clothes are kept in the —— .
9. The coal is kept in the —— .
10. Father keeps his tools in the —— .

Now write at least **ten** sentences about your own home. Mention which rooms you like best, and say why they are your favourites. You can write about the furniture, and any pictures that you are fond of. If you have a cupboard or bookshelf of your very own, mention that too. You can also mention any changes which you wish your parents would make if it was possible.

[68]

48 REVISION

Write one of these words in each of the spaces in the passage which follows. Some must be used more than once:

John said that from the tree —— to the fence over —— was a hundred yards. He asked me to race him —— and back, but I said it was —— far. Then —— of my friends came along, and they happened to —— what we were talking about. They said they would race John, and asked me —— hold —— coats. Then they all dashed towards the fence. John got —— first, but one of my friends passed him just afterwards. Just before the end of the race my other friend passed him —— .

Here is the beginning of a little story. You are given three sentences. Write another **three** sentences of your own, saying what happened next:

John went with his father by car to see a big football match. After the game he somehow lost his father in the crowd. He tried to ask where the car park was, but although this was in England, none of the people he asked to help him seemed to be able to understand English!

[69]

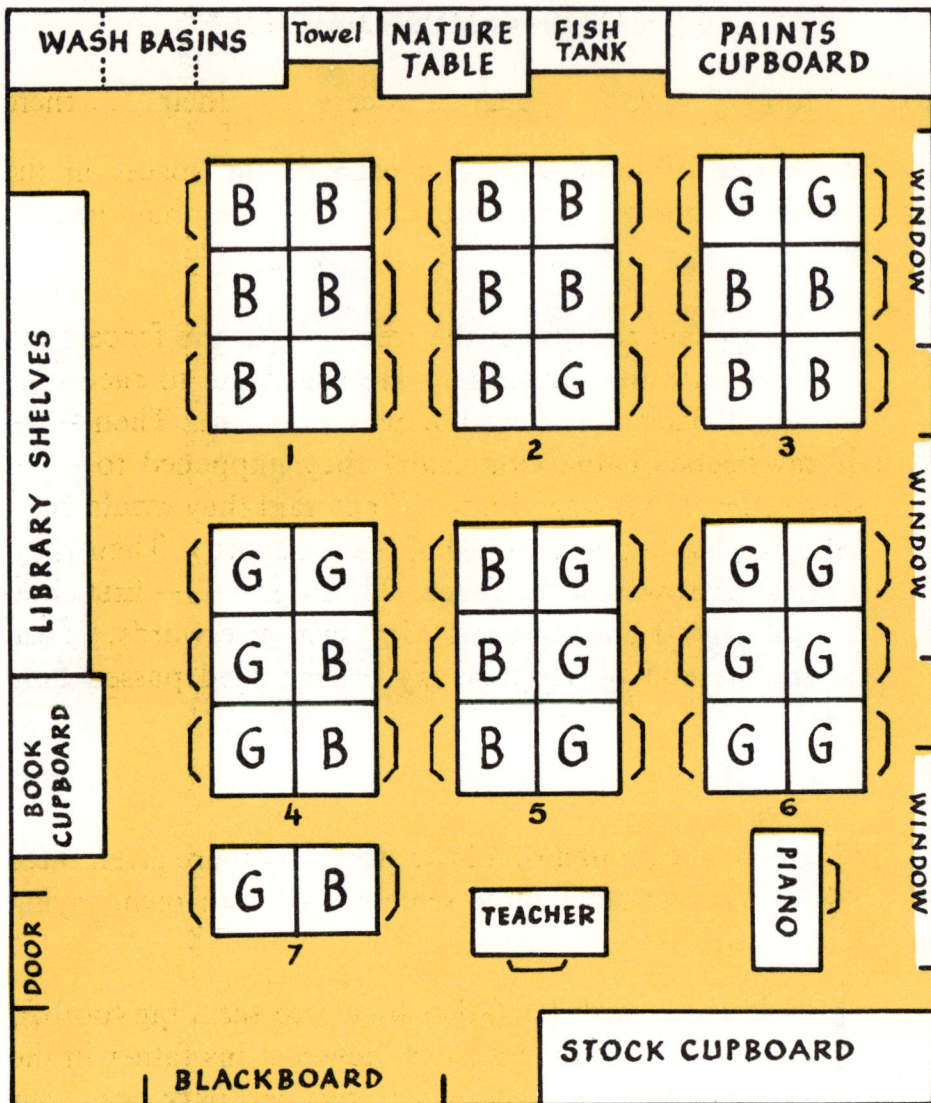

Note that the children's tables are numbered. The letter 'B' or 'G' shows whether a place belongs to a boy or a girl.

[70]

49 IN THE CLASSROOM

Look at the plan of a classroom on the opposite page, and then answer the questions below in **complete sentences.**

1. How many children are there in the class?
2. How many more boys than girls are there?
3. How many windows are there in the classroom?
4. What are the names of the cupboards?
5. At which table do only girls sit?
6. At which table are there twice as many boys as girls?
7. At which tables are there equal numbers of boys and girls?
8. Which is the largest cupboard in the classroom?
9. When the teacher plays the piano, what is behind her?
10. If you came in the door, turned left, and walked straight ahead, what would you come to?

Now write **ten** sentences about **your own** classroom. You may mention how it differs from the one shown here, and draw a plan of it if you have time. You will find the words on the plan helpful.

Now write **one** sentence about each of the children who share your table.

[71]

50 TELLING A STORY

These pictures tell a story. The sentences below tell the same story, but they are in a different order. Write them in the **same order** as the **pictures**:

a. A policeman helped John up.
b. He ran out of the gate and along the road.
c. With its brakes squealing, a car stopped just in time.
d. John's aunt gave him ten new pence.
e. Without stopping, he dashed into the road behind it.
f. He told him to use the zebra crossing and be more careful.
g. John fell over in his panic.
h. There was a car standing by the kerb.

51 SENTENCES IN PAIRS

It was a warm sunny day we decided to have a picnic.

This is **wrong.**   It is written as **one** sentence, but it should be **two** sentences, like this:

It was a warm sunny day.   We decided to have a picnic.

Now divide each of these into **two** sentences:

1. The rain poured down soon there were puddles on the grass.
2. The rocket zoomed up it was out of sight in two minutes.
3. The cat sprang from behind the bush it was just too late.
4. The garden was full of flowers I liked the roses best of all.
5. The cars were in a jam they crept forward every few minutes.
6. The guard blew his whistle the train moved off.
7. We stood on the bridge we watched the trains going beneath us.
8. The mower would not cut the grass it was not sharp enough.
9. It was very hot the ice-cream man soon sold out.
10. The jet roared over the town many people were frightened.

Now write out this passage as **five** sentences, instead of only one as it is here:

The cat is a beautiful animal she loves to sit in front of the fire on cold days when night comes, however, she likes to go out into the darkness then she becomes a cruel hunter it is death for any tiny mouse or shrew that crosses her path.

52 DAYS OF THE WEEK

Solomon Grundy
Born on Monday,
Christened on Tuesday,
Married on Wednesday,
Ill on Thursday,
Worse on Friday,
Dead on Saturday,
Buried on Sunday—
That was the end
Of Solomon Grundy.

Now put the missing letters in these sentences, which tell the same story:

Solomon Grundy was born on M.nday. On the T.esday he was christened. He was married on We.ne.d.y and was taken ill on T.ur.d.y. He became worse on Fr.d.y, and died on Sat..day. He was buried on S.nd.y, and that was the end of him.

Remember that **the days of the week always begin with capital letters.**

This is Susan's diary, showing some of the things she did during the week:

November	November
18 Sunday Rained all day. Went to church.	22 Thursday Played netball at school.
19 Monday Went to Pam's birthday party.	23 Friday Went to Brownies with Pauline.
20 Tuesday Started ballet lessons with Pat.	24 Saturday Went to Auntie Jean's for tea.
21 Wednesday Foggy. Came home early.	Notes: Mum's birthday next Monday.

Now draw a diary for a week like Susan's and try to remember something which happened or which you did on every day last week.

Write out this passage as **four** sentences, putting the missing word in the last sentence:

To-day is Jim's birthday the day before yesterday he slipped and cut his knee as he came out of Sunday School he was able to go to school yesterday, but will not be able to play football to-morrow the day after to-morrow, which is ———, he is having a party.

53 were AND where

Were you able to go to Brownies?
There **were** dark clouds in the sky.
Where is my satchel?
I do not know **where** to go.

These sentences show you how to use **were** and **where**.

Note that **were** rhymes with **sir,** and **where** rhymes with **chair.**

Complete these sentences by putting **were** or **where** in each space:

1. There —— hundreds of birds on the building.
2. —— the bank robbers caught?
3. —— did you put my comic?
4. —— are you going for your holiday?
5. —— the buses on time?
6. I don't know —— John has gone.
7. We —— just in time to see the queen.
8. The birds —— frightened by the gun.
9. Do you know —— I can buy some marbles?
10. —— is the police station?

Now do the same with this passage:

Some people —— standing at the cross-roads—— the accident had happened. Firemen had put sand on the road —— oil had been spilled, and some policemen —— moving the damaged cars to a place —— they would not block the road. The drivers —— shaken but unhurt.

54 WORDS WITH igh

light	sight	might	flight	bright
night	tight	fright	high	fight

Learn how to spell these words.

Now write out these sentences, putting in the missing letters:

1. Sam said his belt was too t . . . t.
2. The crash of thunder gave Pauline a real fr . . . t.
3. John hit the ball with all his m . . . t.
4. The garden was a wonderful s . . . t.
5. Our holiday started on a br . . . t sunny day.
6. The boys had a f . . . t over the marbles.
7. Jane was on a fl . . . t to Scotland.
8. The clouds were very h . . . .
9. It was l . . . t by six o'clock.
10. Did you hear the rain last n . . . t?

Do the same with this passage:

Juliet s . . . ed with del . . . t when she saw the frilly n . . . tgown her mother had bought for her. She held it t . . . tly as she held it up to the l . . . t, as if it m . . . t fly away. "Did you ask if it was all r . . . t, Mummy?" she said. "It's wonderful."

Now write **eight** sentences about some of the best presents that you have ever been given.

[77]

55 NAMES OF THE MONTHS

Copy the names of the months into your book:

January	February	March	April
May	June	July	August
September	October	November	December

They **ALWAYS** begin with a **capital letter.**

Here is an old rhyme to learn:

> Thirty days hath September,
> April, June and November.
> All the rest have thirty-one
> Except February alone,
> Which hath twenty-eight days clear,
> And twenty-nine each leap-year.

Now write out these sentences, putting in the missing letters:

1. Jan.ary, M.rch, M.y and J.ly all have thirty-one days.
2. A.gust, O.tober, and De.ember also have thirty-one days.
3. Apr.l, J.ne, Sep.ember and Nov.mber all have thirty days.
4. The shortest month of the year is Feb.u.ry.

Now write **one** sentence about each of the twelve months. Begin like this:

January is the first month of the year, and is cold.

56 COLOURS

blue	red	green	yellow	purple
black	white	brown	pink	orange

These are the names of **colours.** Write these sentences and put in the missing letters:

1. Wheat turns y . . . . w when it is ripe.
2. The marigolds were a beautiful o . . . . e colour.
3. The rain has made the grass very g . . . n.
4. The sea was a deep b . . e.
5. The fire-engine was painted r . d.
6. Mother picked a p . . k rose.
7. The bride wore a w . . . e dress.
8. The leaves turn b . . . n in autumn.
9. Father bought some b . . . k paint.
10. We ate some juicy p . . . . e plums.

Here are the names of six colours. The letters of each have become mixed up. Can you sort them out?

uleb	teiwh	neegr
kipn	ownbr	kclab

Now write out this passage correctly as **five** sentences:

Each school football team wears the strip of a famous league club one wears the red shirts with white sleeves of Arsenal their nearest neighbours play in the royal blue of Chelsea another school, hoping to have the same success of Leeds United wear an all white strip our own school favours the light blue shirts of Manchester City.

[79]

57 WRITING THE DATE

On the left of the page are some dates.   On the right of the page is the **short** way of writing them:

The first of January	1st January
The second of February	2nd February
The third of April	3rd April
The eighth of June	8th June
The twelfth of August	12th August
The twentieth of November	20th November
The thirtieth of December	30th December

Here is part of a calendar, showing the month of July:

JULY					
Sunday	.	5	12 H	19	26
Monday	.	6 E	13	20	27
Tuesday	.	7	14	21 M	28
Wednesday	1 F	8	15	22 D	29
Thursday	2	9	16 A	23	30
Friday	3	10 J	17	24	31 S
Saturday	4 T	11	18 B	25	.

The letters you can see under some of the numbers in the calendar are the initials of ten children who have their birthdays in July.

Here are the children's names:

Dick	Fred	Jean	Bill	Tom
Susan	Ellen	Mary	Ann	Harry

Write a sentence about each child's birthday in the same order as their names are given above.   Use the **short** form of the date.

Begin like this:

   1.   Dick's birthday is 22nd July.

Now write down the names of children in your class who were born in the same month as yourself, and beside them write the dates of their birthdays.

Now finish this birthday story by adding at least **three** sentences of your own, in which you explain exactly what happened:

It was Helen's eighth birthday, and her party was due to begin at five o'clock. Her mother had prepared a lovely tea complete with jellies, cakes and ice cream. Her father had made up lots of exciting games and had the prizes all ready. But at half past five not one of the invited guests had come.

[81]

58 YOUR HOME

A child was asked these questions about her home:

1. Do you live in a house or a flat?
2. Have you a garden?
3. How many bedrooms are there?
4. Have you a separate dining room and lounge?
5. What other rooms are there?
6. Is there a garage?

Suppose **you** had been asked these questions. Write down the answers **you** would have given.

Later, the child wrote **four** sentences about her home, but she forgot to put in the **full stops,** and the **capital letters** which follow them. Write it out correctly:

This is what she wrote:

I live in a house in Brent Road we have four rooms as well as a kitchen and bathroom at the back of the house is the garden where we play the garage where my father keeps his car is at the side

Now look at the air photograph on the opposite page, which shows a new housing estate. How many different kinds of home can you see? Is there a school, or even two schools? What are the roads like? How do the new homes differ from the older ones? Would you like to live there? Why, or why not?

Think about these questions, then write **eight** sentences about the picture.

59 WORDS ENDING WITH ck AND ke

When a word ends in **ck** the vowel has a **short** sound.
So the word **stack** rhymes with the colour **black.**

When a word ends in **ke** the vowel has a **long** sound.
So the word **make** rhymes with **snow-flake.**

Now write out these sentences, choosing the one correct word from each set of brackets:

1. The (duke   duck) wore red robes.
2. The (duke   duck) swam on the pond.
3. The (coke   cock) crowed loudly.
4. We burn (coke   cock) on the fire.
5. I can (bake   back) cakes.
6. My brother hurt his (bake   back).
7. Put the plates in the (rake   rack).
8. Please (rake   rack) up the leaves.
9. Let's (pike   pick) some wild flowers.
10. My uncle caught a (pike   pick) in the river.
11. The old man lived in a (shake   shack).
12. Will you (shake   shack) the cloth for me?

Now turn either to your reading book or to your dictionary, and find **ten** more words ending in **ck,** and **ten** ending in **ke,** and write them down. See if you can find some more 'pairs' of words, like those used in the exercise above.

[84]

60 PUTTING SENTENCES IN ORDER

Each group of four sentences tells a little story, but the sentences are in the wrong order.   Write out each group of sentences in the **right** order.

1.   The lady took her across when the road was clear.
     Jean was afraid to cross the road.
     Jean thanked her and ran off to the shops.
     She asked a lady to see her across.

Begin this group like this:

   Jean was afraid to cross the road.

2.   Then he looked left, and then to the right again.
     He looked to the right first.
     Jack stopped at the kerb.
     As the road was clear he walked across.

3.   A car which was coming just missed her.
     The ball went into the road and she ran after it.
     She decided never to play ball in the street again.
     Josie ran along the street bouncing a ball.

Now write groups of four sentences **of your own** describing how:

a.   A policeman helped some children across a busy road.

b.   A child had a narrow escape when running across the road to buy an ice-cream from a van.

[85]

61 WORDS ENDING IN f

Some words ending in **f** have **s** on the end to show there is **more than one.**

roof	hoof	chief	dwarf	handkerchief
roofs	hoofs	chiefs	dwarfs	handkerchiefs

Most words ending with **f leave off** the **f** and **add ves** at the ends to show there is **more than one.**

leaf	loaf	half	shelf	wolf	thief	calf
leaves	loaves	halves	shelves	wolves	thieves	calves

Most words ending with **fe** change the **f** to **v** and add **s** to show there is **more than one.**

life	wife	knife
lives	wives	knives

Now write out this passage, changing the words in bold type to show that there is **more than one:**

The hunters heard the howls of the **wolf** coming closer and closer. They took out their **knife** and prepared to fight for their **life.** But then they heard the thunder of **hoof** and a horseman carrying a rifle came galloping through the fallen **leaf.** They waved their **handkerchief,** and he smiled as he reined in his horse. "They will not come near a man with a gun," he said.

Now write a story of your own about as long as the passage above, called "A Narrow Escape."

[86]

62 DESCRIBING WORDS

wide	beautiful	large	old
fast	tall	heavy	deep

These are **describing** words.

Fit each of these words into one of these sentences:

1. Mary has a very b—— garden.
2. The river is very w—— just there.
3. My great-grandfather is o——.
4. Jack's uncle has a f—— sports car.
5. New factories do not have t—— chimneys.
6. The box was so h—— that I could not lift it.
7. The water in that gravel pit is d——.
8. The duke lived in a l—— palace in the country.

Here are some more describing words:

shallow	young	ugly	narrow
short	light	slow	small

These words are the **opposites** of those in the first list.

Now complete these sentences:

1. The opposite of wide is —— .
2. The opposite of heavy is —— .
3. The opposite of old is —— .
4. The opposite of tall is —— .
5. The opposite of deep is —— .
6. The opposite of beautiful is —— .
7. The opposite of fast is —— .
8. The opposite of large is —— .

63 ROAD SIGNS

These are some of the road signs put up to help drivers:

CROSS SCHOOL LEVEL STEEP ROUND-
ROADS   CROSSING HILL ABOUT

BEND DOUBLE HOSPITAL ROAD HUMP
      BEND   NARROWS BRIDGE

Next time you go out in a car or a coach, make a note of all the road signs you see. You should see many more besides those above.

In this story, road signs have been drawn in place of some of the words. Write it out, putting in the words in place of the road signs:

We set out quite early in the morning, and turned

left at the [X] near our house. We went down a

[steep hill] and passed a [school] and a [hospital] . We had

to slow down at a sharp [bend] , and held tight to our

tummies when we crossed a ▢ . Soon we came to a place where the ▢ , and then had to go round a ▢ . After taking the second exit from a ▢ we reached a ▢ . The gates were open, so we went straight on and took the first turning on the right to our aunt's house.

64 MORE SENTENCE BUILDING

lake   **boats**   **small**

The lake was crowded with children in small boats.

The three words in bold type have all been used in the sentence beneath them.

Do the same with these groups of words.   You may use them in any order.

1. picnic   rain   heavy
2. car   ditch   blue
3. chimney   smoke   black
4. flats   block   tall
5. station   train   diesel
6. airport   plane   jet
7. bicycle   shed   new
8. cottage   tiles   green
9. football   match   exciting
10. doll   pram   red

65 OCCUPATIONS

Postman   Dentist   Doctor   Plumber

Dustman   Baker   Milkman   Policeman

Here are the people in the pictures telling you about their work:

a. I leave the milk on your step every morning.
b. I come round with the bread every day.
c. I see you safely across the road.
d. I come to see you when you are ill.
e. I bring letters and postcards to your house.
f. I collect your rubbish every week.
g. I mend your burst pipes in cold weather.
h. I look after your teeth for you.

Write down these sentences in the **same order** as the pictures.

[90]

Now write a story, of about **eight** sentences called "People who come to our house." Of course you can mention some of the people you have just written about, but there must be quite a lot more, including the paper boy or girl, and the scouts and guides who come collecting jumble.

66 JOINING SENTENCES WITH and

Tom likes apples.   Tom likes pears.
Tom likes apples **and** pears.

The first two sentences have been joined into one sentence by using **and.** When two sentences are about things or people which are **alike** in some way, we join them like this.

Do the same with these pairs of sentences:
1.   Mary likes sewing.   Mary likes knitting.
2.   John likes football.   John likes cricket.
3.   I like reading.   I like writing.
4.   Father likes gardening.   Father likes golf.
5.   Mother likes roses.   Mother likes sweet peas.
6.   Lambs are gentle.   Calves are gentle.
7.   Kittens are playful.   Puppies are playful.
8.   Sugar is sweet.   Honey is sweet.
9.   Lilies are white.   Snowdrops are white.
10.   Australia is a big country.   Canada is a big country.

Begin like this:
1.   Mary likes sewing and knitting.

[91]

67 SUMMER AND WINTER

Here are twelve sentences. **Six** of them are about **summer,** and the others are about **winter:**

a. The snow was six inches thick.
b. We skated on the frozen pond.
c. We were glad to sit down in the shade.
d. We had lots of cold drinks.
e. The trees in the park were quite bare.
f. The ice-creams melted before we could eat them.
g. We warmed our hands in front of the fire.
h. The garden was a mass of flowers.
i. It was quite dark when we came out of school.
j. The beach was crowded with sunbathers.
k. We put on our warmest coats and gloves.
l. The sun was very hot indeed.

First write out the six sentences about **summer.** Then write out the six sentences about **winter.** Now write six sentences of your own about **spring.** Here are some useful words:

daffodils	hedgehog	primrose	showers	sunshine	park
leaves	crocuses	cuckoo	swallow	tortoise	nests
garden	violets	picnic	Easter	blossom	frost
country	grass	lambs	clothes	cricket	buds

Many people have written poems about Spring. Try to write one yourself. It need not be long, but try to put into it some of the joy that people, and all living things, feel at this time of year.

[92]

68 JOINING SENTENCES WITH but

Mary likes beef.   She does not like chicken.

Mary likes beef **but** she does not like chicken.

The first two sentences have been made into one sentence by joining them with **but**.   When two things or people are **different** or **opposite**, we join sentences about them with **but.**

Do the same with these pairs of sentences:

1. The deer is timid.   The lion is fierce.
2. Syrup is sweet.   Vinegar is sour.
3. Jean is tall.   Susan is short.
4. Daffodils are yellow.   Forget-me-nots are blue.
5. Mother likes cooking.   She hates darning.
6. Father's car is old.   Uncle's car is brand new.
7. Coal is black.   Snow is white.
8. Summer is warm.   Winter is cold.
9. Cats have smooth coats.   Dogs have rough coats.
10. Some people are rich.   Most people are poor.

Now write down the words in list **a,** and beside each write the word from list **b** which is opposite to it in meaning.

a.	sweet	tame	fresh	black	near
	old	lean	narrow	bright	hard
b.	stale	plump	wide	dull	easy
	white	wild	bitter	young	far

[93]

69 PICTURES AND WORDS

These pictures tell a story about a boy called Jim:

Here are eight sentences which tell the same story, but they are **not** in the right order. Write them out in the **same order** as the **pictures**:

a. He leaned over the water trying to reach his cap with the stick.
b. One day Jim tripped on the river bank and his cap fell in the water.
c. A man hurried up and threw him a lifebelt.
d. He splashed about in the water shouting for help.
e. He wondered how to get it out, and then saw a stick.
f. The man helped him up safely on to the bank.
g. Suddenly he lost his balance and fell in.
h. The frightened boy grabbed the lifebelt and was pulled to the bank.

Of course Jim arrived home soaking wet and very frightened. Write down the story you think he would tell his parents, and say what his parents might say to him when they had heard all about it.

Now write a story of your own describing how a boy or girl was rescued when they were in great danger. Make it about as long as the story above. Your story need not be about someone falling in the water. There are lots of other ways children can get into danger!

[95]

70 REVISION—MORE THAN ONE

Finish these sentences:
1. We say one dog, but many —— .
2. We say one knife, but a set of —— .
3. We say one church, but several —— .
4. We say one chief, but five —— .
5. We say one cherry, but a pound of —— .
6. We say one glass, but a pair of —— .
7. We say one lady, but a team of —— .
8. We say one thief, but a gang of —— .
9. We say one wife, but six —— .
10. We say one fairy, but four —— .

Do it like this:

1. We say one dog, but many dogs.

Now arrange these words into **four columns**, according to whether they end with **es, ies, ves,** or **s** when there is **more than one.**

trolley	loaf	key	bush	remedy	arch
reply	baby	wolf	donkey	shelf	box
chimney	brush	calf	sentry	turkey	glass
thief	country				

Do it like this:

bushes	remedies	loaves	keys
arches	replies	wolves	trolleys

[96]

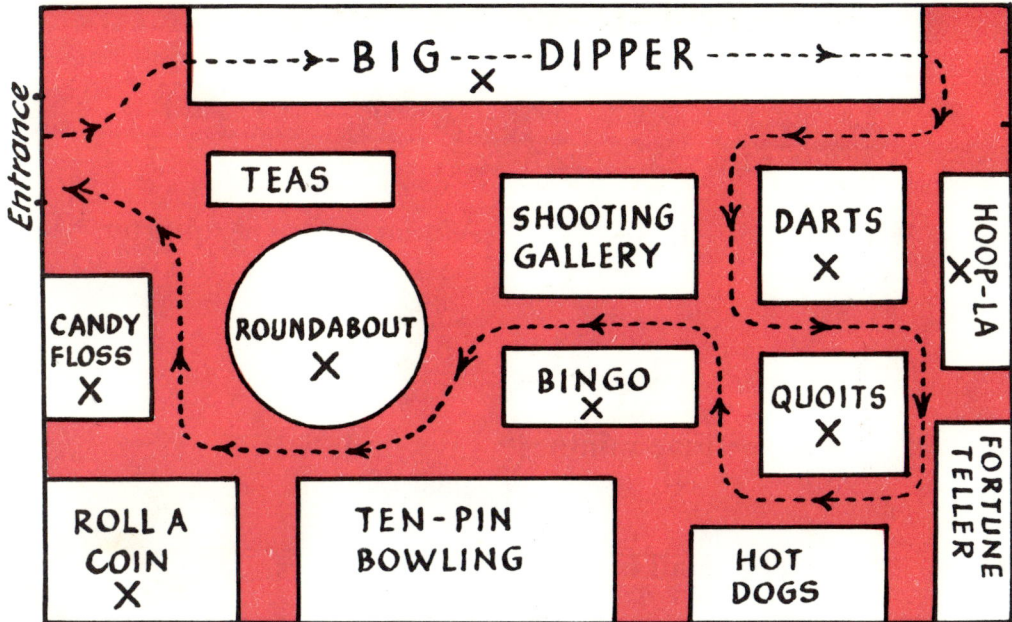

The map shows a funfair layout. Labels read:

Entrance

BIG ---- DIPPER
X

TEAS

SHOOTING GALLERY

DARTS
X

HOOP-LA
X

CANDY FLOSS
X

ROUNDABOUT
X

BINGO
X

QUOITS
X

FORTUNE TELLER

ROLL A COIN
X

TEN-PIN BOWLING

HOT DOGS

71 THE FUN OF THE FAIR

Clive and Joyce went with their father to a funfair. You can see a plan of it above. The dotted line and the arrows show the way they went round. The places where they spent money are marked with a cross.

Now imagine that you are either Clive or Joyce, and write an account of your visit. Make it as interesting and lively as you can. The words on the plan will be useful. Here are some more:

thrills	excitement	colourful	lights	crowds	music
dear	decorations	prizes	noise	skill	showman
glare	smells	money	caravan	lorry	engine

[97]

72 TELLING THE TIME

Three
o'clock

Half-past
one

A quarter
past four

A quarter
to six

Five minutes
to seven

Five minutes
past eleven

The small hand points to the **hours.**

The large hand points to the **minutes.**

Here are some sentences telling you about Tom getting ready for school.

Write them out, putting words instead of the clock-faces.

1. Tom wakes up every morning at

2. He gets up at

3. He is washed and dressed by

[98]

4. At he has his breakfast.

5. He is on his way to school by

6. At exactly he goes in the school gate.

People have not always had clocks to tell the time. Find out what they used in far away times, and think about all the different kinds of clocks and watches that there are to-day. When you have talked about it and thought about it, write **ten** sentences on "Telling the Time."

73 JOINING SENTENCES WITH and OR but

Tom is good at sums.   Harry is good at sums.
Tom **and** Harry are good at sums.

When two sentences are about things or people who are **alike** in some way, we join them with **and.**

Oranges are sweet.   Lemons are sour.
Oranges are sweet **but** lemons are sour.

When two sentences are about things or people who are **different** or **opposite** in some way, we join them with **but.**

Now join these sentences either with **and** or with **but**.

1. John is young.   Grandfather is old.
2. Alan collects stamps.   Paul collects stamps.
3. Tom is at home.   Ronald is on holiday.
4. My blazer is old.   My raincoat is new.
5. I like history.   I like geography.
6. Susan likes potatoes.   Susan likes beans.
7. The Christmas holiday is short.   The summer holiday is long.
8. Mr. Green likes television. Mr. Brown likes television.
9. Our cat likes fish.   He does not like meat.
10. John likes playing ludo. John likes playing cards.

Now write about **eight** sentences about "My friend and I," or "My brother (or sister) and I." Mention the things you both enjoy doing, but also mention the ways in which your likes and dislikes are different.

74 WHERE IS IT?

outside	behind	between	through	under
across	inside	over	towards	into

These words tell you **where things are,** or **where they have gone.**

Take a word from the list to complete each of the sentences below. Each sentence describes one of the pictures. The words in the list are **not** in the right order:

1. The cat is —— the table.
2. The dog is —— his kennel.
3. The car is —— the garage.
4. The sun is —— the church.
5. The boy is —— two girls.
6. The horse jumped —— the hoop.
7. The girl fell —— the river.
8. Jack walked —— the road.
9. Sheila is walking —— the bicycle.
10. Harry hid —— the hedge.

[102]

75 THE DOLPHIN

Read this passage carefully:

Dolphins, which can grow up to 8 feet long, are members of the whale family. They are found in all the world's oceans, and live in families, just as we do. The father is called a bull, the mother a cow, and the babies calves. The family always keep to a territory of about 100 square miles, and never stray from this. As they swim around hunting for fish, led by the bull, they often break the surface of the water, for they are not fish, but air-breathing mammals. Dolphins in captivity are very quick to learn tricks, and to obey a whistle. Of course, as soon as a dolphin has done his act he is rewarded with a fish.

Write out these sentences, putting in the missing words:

1. Dolphins belong to the ——— family.
2. They are not fish but ———.
3. The area where they live is called their ———.
4. Dolphins have to come to the surface to ———.
5. Baby dolphins are called ———.
6. A ——— dolphin always leads his family when hunting.
7. A dolphin's territory is about ——— square miles.
8. A dolphin trainer always uses a ———.
9. After its act a dolphin is ——— with a fish.
10. Dolphins which live in pools and do tricks are in ———.

76 SENTENCES IN TWOS

We went in a speedboat on Saturday it was very exciting.

This is **wrong.** It is written as **one** sentence. It **should** be written as **two** sentences, like this:

We went in a speedboat on Saturday. It was very exciting.

Now write these as two sentences:

1. We saw a good film on television it was about cowboys.
2. I like space stories I think they are very exciting.
3. The diver went down into the sea he came up after ten minutes.
4. It was fun on the roundabouts I liked the swings as well.
5. Father lit the bonfire the flames shot up into the air.
6. There were strong gusts of wind they brought the leaves fluttering down.
7. The sun was very hot it burned our backs quite badly.
8. The knife was sharp it cut through the wood easily.
9. The boy climbed the apple tree he did not see the farmer.
10. The factory caught fire it was soon burned down.

Now write out this passage as **six** sentences, not **one** as it is here:

Cotton is an important clothing material it is obtained from the seed pods of a bush Britain's climate is too cold for it we therefore have to import all we need most of our supplies come from America and Egypt the raw cotton is spun and woven into cloth in Lancashire.

77 WORDS WHICH ASK QUESTIONS

Who was the first man in space?
What did you say?
When did Hillary climb Mount Everest?
Were you late for school yesterday?
Why did you dial 999?
Where did the tug sink?

The words in bold type are often used when **asking questions**.

Now fit one of them into each of these sentences:

1. —— the divers able to find the wreck?
2. —— wrote the poem you have just learned?
3. —— had the plane come from?
4. —— happened when the doctor came?
5. —— is the queen coming to open the motorway?
6. —— did Gagarin make his space flight?
7. —— was the result of the match?
8. —— didn't you meet me yesterday?
9 —— you able to find your library book?
10. —— are you going for your holidays next week?

[105]

78 A BUSY STREET

On the opposite page is a picture of a High Street on Saturday morning. There are streets like this all over Britain though few are as modern as this one in a new town. Look at it carefully and note all the things that are happening. Look at the vehicles, the people, the shops and the bridge for crossing the road. Look at the queues, the lamp-posts and the bus shelters. Think about your own town, as well, and then write **ten** sentences about "A Busy Street."

79 SHOPS

There is a row of six shops in the High Street, and the names of the shopkeepers tell you what they sell. Here they are:

Mr. Bun	Mr. Sweet	Mr. Bacon
Mr. Mutton	Mr. Haddock	Mr. Orange

Now complete the sentences below:
1. The fishmonger is Mr. —— .
2. The butcher is Mr. ——— .
3. The confectioner is Mr. —— .
4. The grocer is Mr. —— .
5. The baker is Mr. —— .
6. The greengrocer is Mr. —— .

Now write **two** sentences about each of the shops on p. 107 and mention some of the things it sells. Make your sentences interesting, and as different from each other as you possibly can. Here are some words which will help you:

lollies	toffees	herrings	potatoes	crab	
meat	bananas	rolls	chops	chocolate	flour
cod	cheese	apples	sausages	lobster	sugar
bread	eggs	ham	fruit	liver	

Now write **eight** sentences about "Shopping with Mother."

80 ANIMALS AT WORK

On the opposite page you can see a picture of an elephant at work in Ceylon. He is clearing the trees away so that crops can be grown. Many other animals work hard in different ways to help us. Among them are dogs, cats, horses and camels. Can you think of any others? Now write a story of at least **ten** sentences called "Animals that help us."

81 is–his   as–has

Tom **is** going to the pantomime on **his** birthday.

This sentence shows you how to use **is** and **his**. Remember that the word **is** is a verb.

Auntie May **has** a dog **as** well **as** a cat.

This sentence shows you how to use **as** and **has**. Remember that the word **has** is a verb.

Now write out these sentences, putting the right word in each space:

1. Frank had a tear in —— best coat.
2. Jack hit the ball —— far —— he could.
3. The pilot lost —— way over the Alps.
4. The lion —— far stronger than the horse.

5. The dog slipped —— collar.
6. The cat —— sharp claws.
7. She shouted —— she fell over.
8. I don't know if she —— any money.
9. Sheila —— coming to tea soon.
10. He ducked —— head —— the ball flew towards him.

82 is–was are–were

Peter **is** clever.   John and Simon **are** twins.
Susan **was** first.   Jill and Pauline **were** late.

Is and **was** are used when writing about **one** person or thing.
Are and **were** are used for **more than one.**

Now put the missing word into these sentences:
1. Harry and Jim —— going to church to-morrow.
2. Mary —— hoping for a baby sister soon.
3. The dog —— barking last night.
4. All the planes —— grounded by fog yesterday.
5. The two children —— playing a duet to-night.
6. Tim —— away from school last week.
7. The boys —— thrilled when the footballers spoke to them.
8. The queen —— visiting Manchester next spring.
9. All the horses —— jumping well at yesterday's show.
10. Beethoven —— deaf for many years.

Put **is** or **are** in each of the spaces in the following passage:

Peter —— learning the recorder, and John —— having lessons on the piano. Their cousins Janet and Susan —— both learning the violin. They —— all at the same school, and their teacher —— hoping to put on a concert soon. All the children —— practising hard, but Peter —— very keen indeed. He and his brother and cousins —— going to do extra practice before the concert.

Have you ever been in a play or a music concert at school? Write an account of it, and mention all the hard work that has to be done before the day of the performance.

83 ANSWERING QUESTIONS

The picture shows some children enjoying a party. You can see their names.

Fred   Sheila   Harry

Tom   Susan

Jane   Dick   Mary

[111]

Now answer each of these questions in a complete sentence:

1. Who is sitting opposite Susan?
2. Which boys are sitting between two girls?
3. Which boy is sitting nearest to Susan?
4. Which girls are sitting between two boys?
5. Which girl is sitting nearest to Tom?
6. Which boy is sitting nearest to Fred?
7. Who is sitting opposite to Fred?
8. Which girl is sitting nearest to Susan?
9. Which boy is sitting nearest to Tom?
10. Which girl is sitting nearest to Mary?

Answer like this:

1. Tom is sitting opposite Susan.

Children at parties have great fun playing games, and have delightful things to eat and drink. Think about some of the parties you have been to, and write about them. Mention games, food, and anything unexpected that happened. Write about **eight** sentences.

Now write this passage correctly as **six** sentences:

Susan's party was a great success it was different from most other parties too soon after the first guest arrived all the lights went out there had been a fault at the power station however everyone enjoyed the soft flickering yellow candlelight the electricity did not come on until the party was nearly over.

Look at this picture of a great modern airliner. It could fly to almost any part of the world in a couple of days. Imagine that you are just about to board it for a long and exciting journey. Describe your flight and the interesting places you saw, and write about the adventures you had when you reached your destination.

The photograph above is of a Boeing 707 airliner owned by B.O.A.C. In the background you can see a V.C. 10 airliner. See how many other kinds of aeroplane you can find out about. There are lots to be found in books and magazines. Make a list of them.

[113]

85 WORDS WHICH SOUND THE SAME

We had **meat** and potatoes for dinner.
I will **meet** you at the school gate.

Meat and **meet** sound the same, but they have **different meanings.**

Here are some more words like this:

fair	steel	sale	pail	hare
fare	steal	sail	pale	hair

Put the missing letters in the spaces in these sentences:
1. There is a fa.. on the common.
2. The bus fa.. to school is two new pence.
3. The helmet was made of st..1.
4. The thief tried to st..1 a purse.
5. The house next door is for sa...
6. My yacht has a blue sa...
7. A pa.. of milk was knocked over.
8. Harry looked pa.. after eating too many cakes.
9. The dog chased the ha...
10. Jill has long brown ha...

Here are some more pairs of words of the same kind:

blue	right	flower	bear	grate	mail
blew	write	flour	bare	great	male

Use each of the words in a short sentence which shows that you understand its meaning.

[114]

86 A PICTURE STORY

These pictures tell how a boy's sensible action saved somebody's life. Write one sentence about each picture, describing what is happening. Try to begin each sentence differently, and avoid using the same words too often.

Begin like this:

Tom set out for school one day

Now write a story of your own, also **eight** sentences long, describing how a girl saw some boys stranded half-way up a cliff. Say how she gave the alarm, and how they were rescued.

87 WHERE DOES IT BELONG?

Write out these words, choosing the correct words from the brackets:

1. Mother boils the water for tea in the (saucepan kettle).
2. Father filled the coal (scuttle bunker) and brought it into the house.
3. Mother had some silver and bronze coins in her (purse wallet).
4. When I go shopping I always take a (suitcase basket).
5. My aunt filled the (bag caddy) with tea.
6. Father always keeps some pound notes in his (pocket wallet).
7. When we wash up we put the plates in the (rack larder) to drain.
8. I always fill the milk (jug churn) before we start tea.
9. My brother has a(n) (book album) in which he keeps foreign stamps.
10. Mary carries her plimsolls and homework books in her (satchel handbag).

These things often go together in **pairs.** Arrange them in these pairs **as sensibly as you can:**

chips	fork	tie	custard	butter
pepper	pen	socks	bread	knife
pencil	collar	fruit	bacon	fish
comb	egg	salt	shoes	brush

Begin like this:
fish and chips.   knife and fork.

88 TWO TOWNS

Details	Extown	Whytown
Population	19,000	25,000
Distance from London	196 miles	75 miles
Early Closing Day	Wednesday	Thursday
Market Day	Friday	Tuesday
Main Industry	Coal Mining	Printing
Places of Interest	Roman Villa, Museum	Art Gallery, Cathedral

Above you can see some details of two towns as shown by a motorist's guide.

Now answer each of these questions about the towns in a complete sentence:

1. Which town has the larger population?
2. Which town is nearer to London?
3. When is it Market Day in Extown?
4. Which town has Early Closing on Wednesday?
5. In which town can you see a Roman Villa?

[117]

6. How many people live in Whytown?
7. Which town has its Market Day earlier in the week?
8. In which town do many miners live?
9. Which are the main places of interest in Extown?
10. In which town can a collection of paintings be seen?

89 MORE THAN ONE

man	foot	tooth	goose	child	ox	sheep
men	feet	teeth	geese	children	oxen	sheep

These words do not follow a rule when we have to show that there is **more than one.**

Write out these sentences, changing the word in bold type—if necessary—to show that there is **more than one**

1. My **foot** hurt after walking two kilometres.
2. The **goose** hissed when anyone went near them.
3. The **mouse** scampered into their holes.
4. The **child** cheered when they were given an extra holiday.
5. The **sheep** were rounded up by the shepherd's dog.
6. The cart was pulled by a team of **ox** .
7. The **man** streamed out of the football ground.
8. The boxer had three **tooth** knocked out.

[118]

90 YOURSELF AND OTHERS

Me and my brother went to the library.

This sentence is **wrong** for **two** reasons:
1. When writing of yourself and another person, the **other person** is **always** mentioned **first.**
2. **Me** is the **wrong** word.   **I** should be used instead. **Never** begin a sentence with **me.**

My brother and I went to the library.
This sentence is right.

Here is another example:
Me and my friend play cricket   —   Wrong
My friend and I play cricket   —   Right

Now write out these sentences as they **should** be written. Remember the **two** mistakes in each which you have to put right.
1. Me and my sister have lots of comics.
2. Me and you can play chess.
3. It is time me and you had a turn on the swings.
4. Perhaps me and you can get into the football team.
5. Me and Jack have each gone up a class.
6. It will be fun if me and you can go to the circus.
7. Me and you can join the Cubs when we are eight.
8. If me and my sister bring our dolls, we can have a party.
9. Me and Fred are going to play marbles.
10. Me and Janice want to be nurses when we grow up.

[119]

91 BIRDS IN THE GARDEN

This is a photograph of some baby robins who are just fourteen days old. They have left the nest, and are about to learn to fly.

Many children, and grown-ups as well, get a lot of pleasure from watching birds even if it is only those in the garden. Think about birds very carefully, and then write at least **ten** sentences about "The Birds in my Garden," or "The Birds in the Park."

When you have written your story, try and write a short poem about birds. It could be about a particular kind of bird, like the robins above, or about birds in general.

92 KEEP DEATH OFF THE ROAD

Below are some sentences which are divided into two parts. The second halves of the sentences have become mixed up. Find the second part of each sentence which begins on the left, and write the sentences out **as they should be:**

1. In the street, keep your dog   into or across the road.

2. People on foot should use   in the street.
3. Never, never run   traffic lights.
4. Read and learn the   wet weather.
5. Never get on or off a bus at   zebra crossings.
6. Boy and girl cyclists should give   on a lead.
7. Take extra care in   Highway Code.
8. Never play games   clear signals.

Do it like this:
1. In the street, keep your dog on a lead.

Below are five boys' names with jumbled letters. Find out what they are and write them down:

ILNCO   NOHJ   KANRF   HELAIMC   UPAL

Now do the same with these girls' names:

CYNAN   ORALC   NSSUA   NLEEH   RYAM

Now sort out the names of these animals:

TGAO   BREA   ERSHO   BEZAR   TARBIB

[121]

HOW MUCH HAVE YOU LEARNED?
SET 1

A. Write out these sentences correctly. There is **one** mistake in each:

    1. Tom is saving up to buy a football
    2. the handle of my shopping bag broke.
    3. What did the doctor say to-day
    4. how many runs did Keith get?
    5. We were late because the bus broke down

B. Put the missing letters in these sentences:

    1. How mu.. are the goldfi.. please?
    2. We sat on the bea.. watching the ..ips.
    3. The b..d was perched on a milk ch..n.
    4. The g..l fell over and h..t her knee.
    5. The str..ts in our town are always cl..n and tidy.

C. Write out these sentences, changing the word in **bold type** to show that there is **more than one**:

    1. We have plenty of **flower** out now.
    2. There is a family of **fox** in High Wood.
    3. We often play noughts and **cross** .
    4. Our team won all their **match** last year.
    5. There are **dash** in place of some of the words.

D. Write out these sentences, putting either **a** or **an** in the spaces:

1. On —— Saturday last year we had —— outing to the Zoo.
2. We each had —— apple and —— cup of tea.
3. —— elephant and —— seal took part in the circus.
4. Tom said he saw —— owl catch —— mouse.
5. ——ash tree and —— birch tree were struck by lightning.

SET 2

A. Write out these sentences, changing **small** letters to **capital** letters where necessary:

1. Did you meet mary yesterday?
2. My cousin lives in yorkshire.
3. I met a boy named john atwell on holiday.
4. Paul has a cat called nigger.
5. We saw a car race at brighton.

B. Put the missing letters in these sentences:

1. Pamela is e...t years old and Jean is f..r.
2. S.v.n rhymes with el...n.
3. Paul hit the ball r...t out of s...t.
4. We watched the bri..e from behind a he..e.
5. You must find a stre..h of level ground for your cricket ma..h.

[123]

C. Change the words in bold type to show that there is more than one:

    1.   The **boy** had lots of **toy** between them.
    2.   Do not let the **baby** eat any of those **berry** .
    3.   There are **donkey** and **monkey** in Pets' Corner.
    4.   Some English **city** have buildings twenty **storey** high.
    5.   Very young children love **story** about **fairy** .

D. Write out these sentences, choosing the correct words from the brackets:

    1.   (There   Their) are no white roses (here   hear).
    2.   Noah had (to   too   two) (of   off) each kind of animal in the Ark.
    3.   I (here   hear) that Fred fell (of   off) his bicycle.
    4.   It is (to   too   two) wet (to   too   two) play cricket.
    5.   Jean and Mary took (there   their) dolls (to   too   two) school.

SET 3

A. Choose the correct word from the brackets in these sentences:

    1.   Put the garden (rake   rack) (bake   back) in the shed.

2. Do you (like   lick) roast (duke   duck) for dinner?
3. Do you know (where   were) the hammer is?
4. The roses (where   were) late coming out this year.
5. (Where   were) does your grandmother live?

B. Write the name of a month or a day of the week in each space below:

1. The first month of the year is —— .
2. The shortest month of the year is —— .
3. The day before Sunday is —— .
4. After Tuesday comes —— .
5. Schools close for summer holidays during —— .

C. Write out these sentences, changing the word in bold type to show that there is more than one:

1. King Henry VIII had six **wife** .
2. Many **roof** lost tiles during the gale.
3. Thousands of **leaf** came fluttering down.
4. The natives all carried long **knife** .
5. Mother asked the baker for two **loaf** .

D. Write out these sentences, putting in the missing words:

1. The Union Jack is red, —— and —— .
2. Knives, forks, and spoons are called —— .
3. Cups, saucers, and plates are called —— .
4. Mother hangs her dresses in the —— .
5. If you mix red and yellow you get —— .

[125]

SET 4

A. These sentences tell you what Pam did each morning, but they are in the **wrong** order. Write them out in the **right order**:

    a.   Then she went downstairs and had her breakfast.
    b.   She then went into the bathroom and washed.
    c.   Pam's mother woke her at half-past seven.
    d.   At a quarter to nine she set off for school.
    e.   A few minutes later she got out of bed and dressed herself.

B. Write out these sentences as they should be, correcting the **two** mistakes in each:

    1.   I am going to see Kent and surrey play cricket
    2.   Peter and jane are having a party to-morrow
    3.   at what time do the shops open
    4.   Did you spend a week at hastings
    5.   Christopher columbus discovered america in 1492.

C. Join each of these pairs of sentences into a **single** sentence by using either **and** or **but**:

    1.   Mary is Scottish.   Olwen is Welsh.
    2.   India is a hot country.   Malaysia is a hot country.
    3.   The Thames is a river.   The Severn is a river.
    4.   Bacon comes from the pig.   Mutton comes from the sheep.

5. Slate is hard.   Chalk is soft.

D. Below are some clock faces.   Write down the time which is shown in each.

SET 5

A. Write out these sentences, putting a suitable verb in each space:

   1. Most of the chimneys in the town were . . . . .
   2. George was . . . . to school when he tripped over.
   3. Jack had a fine time . . . . at the baths.
   4. Peter was scolded for . . . . stones.
   5. As the weather was dry, Susan spent an hour . . . . the garden.

B. Write out these sentences, putting in the missing words:

   1. New Year's Day is the —— of January.
   2. The last day of June is the —— .

3. Christmas Day comes on the —— —— of December.
4. There were eleven children in front of Geoffrey, so he came —— .
5. The middle day of August is the —— .

C. The sentences below are wrong. Each should be written as **two** sentences instead of **one.** Write them out as they should be:
1. Michael picked up his pencil he began to draw.
2. We got up early it was a fine sunny morning.
3. We drank our milk we put the bottles back in the crate.
4. The rain stopped the puddles quickly dried up.
5. The driver braked very hard he just missed the child.

D. Write out these sentences, choosing the correct words from the brackets:
1. The (fare   fair) to London is fifty new pence.
2. My mother bought a coat at a (sail   sale).
3. I was sent out to buy a bag of (flower   flour).
4. Bicycles have strong (steal   steel) frames.
5. The farmer brought us a (pail   pale) of milk.

ACKNOWLEDGMENTS

Acknowledgments are due to the following for supplying photographs for inclusion in this book:

B.O.A.C; John Topham Ltd.; Commission for the New Towns, Hemel Hempstead; G. E. Wheeler, F.Z.S.; Paul Popper Ltd.; David Davies; George Wimpey & Co. Ltd.; Greater London Council Photographic Library; Camera Press Ltd.; Jack Curtis, Reveille.